STEPHONISMS

MY THOUGHTS, MY WORDS, AND MY EXPERIENCES

STEPHON WILLIAMS

For information contact:
http://www.stephonwilliams.com

Cover design by MelindaMartin.me

Edited by Blake Atwood
with BA Writing Solutions LLC
http://www.blakeatwood.com

ISBN: 978-0-578-40753-1

First Edition: December 2018

This book is dedicated to my mother,
Irene Williams,
who has taught me
what unconditional love is.

CONTENTS

INTRODUCTION

Some may not understand my drive to help others or agree with how I see things, but I accept it as part of my journey.

I never felt like I was part of "the group," and I lived with the outside-looking-in perspective. I learned a lot by being observant and quiet during my early years and found that I was being prepared for this work in my later years.

We all have a role to play in this game called life, but, if you don't know the rules, chances are you will feel like life cheated you.

There is a message in your struggle and a purpose in your pain.

—Stephon

MIND-SET

Thoughts are like anchors and balloons so be mindful of the ones you hold onto.

Many of us move through life without understanding the true power our thoughts have over our lives. However, the universal truth is that you have dominion over the thoughts you choose to entertain.

You can focus on thoughts that uplift you or the ones that bring you down. It's your choice of what direction you'll go.

The gift
that people
rarely open is
the mind.

If you don't have a vision for your future, your past will always be your present.

There can be no change without a change of mind. We are creatures of habit and follow the well-worn path of our past, which delivers the same results.

In our personal and professional lives, we must closely examine our goals and ensure our actions align with our desired outcomes.

Failure to do so will surely present your past in your present.

I think,

so I am,

and what I thought,

I became.

A new mind-set creates new outlets for
opportunities.

Can'ts become cans.
Won'ts become wills.
Nos become yeses.

When we change the way we think of things,
those things we think of change.

Am I going through a hard time, or am I being
prepared for something bigger?

It's all a matter of perspective, and your
perspective is based on your mind-set.

Work hard to shape your internal view into
what you want and it will show you what you
must do.

Be mindful of

what you tell yourself

as it becomes

a part of you.

To change your circle of influence, you must first change your mind about what you will and will not accept from life. Then let the universe do the rest.

So many people are stuck in their boxes of misery, it's hard for them to believe anyone else could be happy about life or even optimistic about their future endeavors.

Limit your exposure to these emotional vampires and connect with people who are doing great things and have empowering energy.

You don't have to know them personally. Social media has increased our ability to connect with like-minded people.

We receive

the measure of what

we think of ourselves

and life.

The mind is the projector of life.

To understand the mind, you must study it. Once you understand it, you can employ your mind in your favor to create the life you desire.

You are not hopeless or helpless until you accept it in your mind. Everything begins and ends in the mind.

Either you control it or someone else will.

When you lack
knowledge and
understanding,
you are easily misled
by ignorance.

The mind holds the key!

Your thoughts govern your life; however, you allow your thoughts to be manipulated by people and situations. Once you understand this universal truth and take ownership of your thoughts, you are now in control of change.

Overthinking is the biggest dream killer because nothing leaves the world of thought.

My mind-set is the result of a plan set in motion for success. You must first see and believe before you receive.

If you truly desire success in life, you must see in detail what that looks like.

You must also believe you can obtain those things and that you deserve them.

Lastly, do what must be done to receive your just due.

You beat a dead horse when you don't think he's dead.

Your mind-set determines how much success you will experience in your future.

If you look at change as a bad thing and hold onto things that aren't relevant in the present, it will be difficult to find peace of mind or success in life.

Embrace change and remain relevant, reliable, and ready.

Personal growth is a choice.

Sometimes
things you don't know
control how you think.

You must envision in
your mind and feel in
your heart what you
want to be, and,
once you align your
behavior with it,
so will you see.

Your day, your *now* moment, will be how you choose to see it. Yesterday is gone, so leave it be. Take charge of your thoughts and project on this day what will bring you peace of mind.

When the mind has been conditioned to believe that some things are bigger than they really are, you will forever be stuck if you remain tied to them.

SCIENCE OF SELF

You can't be blessed
until you get rid of your mess.

Many people wish to be blessed but are not willing to remove the things in their lives that prevent new things from manifesting.

They hold on to habits, friends, and mind-sets that keep them anchored in place.

When you remove the old, you make room for the new.

If you are given something to say, say it. If you are given an experience, learn from it. If what you've learned reveals your gift, share it.

If you don't see the problem, you will never get the answer.

What prevents you from being successful is you. Self-defeating behaviors are hidden in your blind spots. But, if you take the effort to turn around and look at yourself objectively, you can minimize the damage you've caused your self-esteem.

- Do you start things but never finish?
- When things seem to be going well, do you start to think the worse?
- Do you desire to be in a healthy relationship but find all the reasons not to, or even treat the person badly so they can leave you?

These are just a few examples.

Find your purpose and it will put you in place to do your part.

Self-improvement is an ongoing and daunting process because it encompasses your shifting paradigms.

This can be much for many. Why?

We become comfortable with our pain, rationalize our failures, and our negative experiences and thoughts dominate our minds.

However, you hold the key to your freedom in your mind: your power to think!
Thoughts become things, people!

You can create a whole new life with different thinking. This is a *fact*.

It's challenging, but the rewards outweigh the efforts.

Being open to unlearn and eager to reexamine your beliefs changes the trajectory of your life.

It's what you don't know that prevents your growth.

What keeps one from advancing in business is a lack of knowing:

- how to navigate your environment
- how to communicate
- how to network
- how to build and maintain relationships
- how to think outside the box
- how to organize
- how to prioritize
- how to choose allies

Don't let where you are now deter you from working toward where you want to be.

The only things you are scared to lose are the things you don't believe you deserve to have.

If something or someone is authentically connected with you, there's a sense of security. When the connection is disingenuous, there's always an air of doubt.

In a relationship, you can ask yourself: Did I force the union? Did I believe I could make them feel like I felt?

Authentic connections are mutually expressed in words and actions, in and out of the presence of the person and in good and bad times.

The difference between authentic and artificial connections is that authenticity gets better through trials and tribulations and artificiality rapidly dissipates in those times.

If you don't like
the reflection in the
mirror, you won't like
what your life
reflects upon you.

Looking to be loved when there is no love within is like looking to fill your cup with a hole in it. There is nothing to sustain what's being received.

If you don't possess love for self, how can you accept love from someone else?

No matter what they do, it will never be enough. You'll question all their motives because, deep down, you believe you don't deserve to be loved.

I put *me* before everything. If I'm not straight, I'm no good for anyone who depends on me. That's not selfish; that's self-prepared.

Your character is found in the details of your actions.

When you truly look, listen, and learn from your experiences, you make wise choices.

You are the gardener of your life; thus, you must know the difference between a flower and a weed.

One brings life; one takes it.

Being open

to question

what you

think you know

is when you prime

yourself to grow.

If our life is a movie, why don't we play the role of the hero or heroine?

All of us at some time played or pretended to be someone like we've seen in the movies or on stage. It empowered us to be something bigger than ourselves.

Why don't we use that same imagination and focus and become the best version of ourselves?

From rags to riches, from victim to victor—if you can choose to be who you want, then choose to be the better you, no matter what your past was.

Don't wait to be cast. Start your independent biopic now with a beautiful ending.

The more I learn about myself, the more I understand about others. The more I learn about life, the more I realize I have to learn to unlearn what I thought I knew.

When you wake up, you have a choice of what face you want to put on, the state of mind you want to be in. You are the maker of your day. Just know that your day is reflected in your face and projected by your mind.

Sometimes we have to leave what we've outgrown in order to have room to grow.

The heart will blind you,

but your mind

will find you.

Don't let your doubt count you out. It's only a sign that what you seek is on the other side of it. You can have it if you feel you deserve it. That thought is a choice.

If you want to change, you have to be willing to change the way you think.

Unprocessed pain leaves recurring stains on our lives. Covering it up won't make it go away. You must examine your life from the inside out, and sometimes you may need assistance in understanding the pieces that are out of place.

I learned not to set unrealistic expectations but to allow myself to be surprised.

You must love yourself first in order to have a fruitful relationship.
If you don't, you will always seek to be loved and never feel loved enough.

If you don't control your pleasure principles, pleasure will control your principles.

If you want to know
why you do
certain things,
examine your past.

MANIFEST

Every door isn't meant for you.

Though you may think at the moment you are ready, what's unknown to you is what lies behind that door.

Many times, I've thought I was ready for what I wanted, but, in actuality, I was not prepared for what I needed.

Why? Because what I needed came with trying tests and sacrifices.

These things were needed to make me, not break me.

When I became appreciative of the doors that were opened to me, I realized that, if I had been allowed to skip some of life's doors, I would have been lost in the corridors of despair, depression, and confusion.

In each room of life, there's a test. If you can't pass the test, you will repeat it.

Seek to recognize and understand unproductive life cycles (recurring pain and problems), then act to change them.

Behind every lesson there's a blessing.

There's no
hocus-pocus,
only hard work
and a purpose.

Emotionalized thoughts

become your reality.

Just because you haven't found your purpose doesn't mean you don't have one.

When your life is full of clutter, it's hard to see what's right in front of you.

Start picking up the pieces instead of staring at them and you will be surprised by what you will find.

In equal measure,
whatever you desire
craves your attention
and company.

I didn't forget where I came from. I just can't stay there.

When you have broadened your perspective of self and the world, it's hard to remain content with each stage of life.

During those stages, there's either growth or stagnation.

If there's growth, you will outgrow people, habits, places, and life's circumstances. If there's stagnation, things remain the same.

Not extracting life lessons from these stages steals one's love for life, thrusting them into darkness.

Seek blessings in the lessons.

Be patient
with those
still processing
their experience.

You will catch
what you pitch.

Patience is

the enemy of gluttons

and a friend

to the successful.

Make the best of your
moments with loved
ones. Live with no
regrets, resentments, or
"I wish I could haves".
Live with love,
understanding,
and forgiveness.

This is a universal truth that many find themselves wrestling with: like attracts like. Alignment is the key to success and failure.

There are no accidents. There is no such thing as luck. It's either that you didn't pay attention or you were prepared for the opportunity.

There are lessons

in your losses.

When you are aware
that life is to be
learned, then you will
recognize that trials
and tribulations
are tests.

When things happen unexpectedly, you must act extraordinarily to the change. This will bring you extraordinary results.

Lessons that make you laugh are kept in your heart.

When you can't; smile.

When you must; laugh.

I can't
change
the weather,
but I can
dress for it.

Our work is reflected

in the lives

of the people

we have touched.

Follow your passion
and it will lead you
to your purpose.

Your faith

will light your way

in the darkness.

People will find

what they want in you,

even if it's not there.

You must see it to be it.

You must believe it
to achieve it.

Focus your energy on situations you can influence; anything else is wasted attention.

You can be

what you want to be

when you decide

to be it.

Your dreams will set

your course, but only

your action

can get you there.

Be what they do not have, do what was not done, and take them where they have not been.

If you want to grow,

you must learn.

If you want to learn,

you must listen.

If you want to

understand,

you must see.

You have to be willing
to be uncomfortable
to live a life
that's memorable.

Your problems are like toddlers. If you don't take care of them, they will cry out until you do.

Inside every person, there is a seed of greatness, but if the soil it resides in fails to be cultivated by life's lessons, the seed will remain buried beneath the fears, doubts, and failures of an unexamined life.

Living your best life

means weathering

doubt and negativity

with optimism,

knowing that

the best is yet to come.

Laughter is

detox

for the soul.

It's good to know where you've come from, but it is also good to know where you are going. You are bigger than where you are now in life, but you must believe it to reveal it.

MOTIVATION

Failure scared me so much it ran me into my purpose.

When failure isn't an option, you will find what's truly hidden inside of you. It's amazing what we can do when our back is against the wall.

There's an energy we will tap into, to get it done. That energy is designed for a purpose, but we must employ it properly. That energy is what we call *spirit.*

Your service or product
must be monetized
if you want to thrive.

Inquire to learn,

develop empathy

to understand,

and take action to fix.

The Marine Corps taught me that every detail counts, and, if not properly addressed, they can distort the bigger picture. Every thought, every decision, and every action taken are comprised of many contributing factors we call details.

Whether it be strategic organizational initiatives or personal matters, the outcomes are governed by the details. If your team seems to be underperforming or your relationship struggling, chances are something is going unnoticed or being mistaken as a nonissue.

Let your past propel you into your future, not hold you there.

So many people allow their pasts to hold them hostage, which prevents them from achieving or envisioning a prosperous future.

They want to move forward, but they won't let go of the fears and pains of the past.

For every mistake you've made, there is a lesson learned.

Victims live in the past while victors make it past.

Your mind-set is a choice. You either choose to remain a victim or become a victor over your situation.

Success comes
in increments,
which add up
if you don't give up.

*When they said, "I can't do that," I said, "I can!"
When they said, "I wouldn't do that," I said, "I
will!" When they said, "It won't work," I said, "It
did!"*

The worst thing you can do to yourself is to let
"them" influence your decisions.

You see, "they" are underachievers and
unbelievers in themselves. "They" project
their insecurities and inadequacies on others
because they don't want to be left behind.

For every goal, "they" may have a rebuttal as
to why you shouldn't pursue it. The biggest
fear for "them" is to see someone do what
"they" want to do and being exposed for not
having what it takes to get it done.

Once you accomplish your goals, "they" will
always find a way to criticize and minimize
your work. Don't be discouraged. This is a sign
that you are moving in the right direction.
Embrace the process of success.

You may

take a few losses,

but your wins

make up for it.

Many entrepreneurs want the success but don't embrace the process.

There will be ups and downs; you just can't stay down.

When a door closes, knock on another one. When they say no, know *someone* will say yes!

There will be some down time, but you have to stay up on your game. Stay the course and stay encouraged.

What you did before
won't give you the
same results today.
To be successful,
reinventing yourself is
essential to thriving
in an ever-changing
tapestry.

Your goal should be to better yourself, not to become someone else.

If you do strive to become someone else, you become an impersonator, an imposter, and a fraud. It's OK to use others as motivation to find your true self, but it's not cool to become somebody else.

Challenge yourself daily to be better in the small things and, over time, you will be whom you were born to be.

Work on

your short gains

as you build for

your big wins.

Your brand is validated by the quality and craftsmanship of your life's garment.

How people feel when they come in contact with you and the impression you leave upon them is your brand.

Your name and everything associated with your name is your brand.

How you communicate, interact, conduct business, and manage relationships establishes your brand (name).

What do you want your brand to be known for?

A key to success is to give more than what is asked for and to be more than what they expected.

If you don't know
what you want to do,
try something until
you find something.

Time is too valuable to be wasted, so make sound investments with your time. If you want your dream to work, you must network till your feet hurt. Don't wait for them to come to you. Go out and get them.

First impressions matter, so strive to be your best you at all times.

In your quest for success in business, relationships, or life, you must allow time to cultivate it. The gestation period is extremely important in the growth of all things. Be patient.

What I was then
doesn't limit what I am
now. It just adds validity
to the journey
of transformation.

Work hard; plan smart; create options. There's nothing more powerful than the power of thought with motivated effort behind it. Many of your opportunities are reflections of your efforts.

Your grind

will cut a path

to your success.

I'm in the business of connecting people, and connected people are more productive, focused, and successful in their pursuit of a goal.

Take your dream

seriously and

your dream

will take you places.

You are

one step

from greatness

once you sidestep

your doubt.

Believe in yourself, even when no else does. The worst thing you can do is to let yourself down. Having a healthy sense of self is one of the keys to success.

Nobody

can do *you*

like you do *you*.

The more *you* do you,

the more *you*

you'll find in *you*.

If you see yourself accomplishing little goals more frequently, you will develop a positive, successful mind-set.

Winning

is struggling

until the goal

is reached.

Don't let doubt
count you out
on your success
or someone else
will count you in
on achieving theirs.

A vision

without action

is just

a dream.

When your hard work
meets its purpose,
people call you
lucky.

Your mind-set
determines your assets.
If your thoughts are of
poverty, so shall it be.
If your thoughts are
of success,
so shall you see.

Act on your dreams
and don't stop
till they become
reality.

D.R.E.A.M. means

Divine

Reality

Eagerly

Awaiting

Manifestation.

Trusting the process is trusting that all things will fall in place when you align yourself with your dream's journey.

I'd been asked numerous times when I would have an open training event. September 9 was the original date, and all of my seats were filled at a beautiful hotel on the beach.

Then Hurricane Irma came, and I had to reschedule and evacuate my family.

I said, "Oh well. Everything happens for a reason."

I returned, thinking it would be easy to reschedule, but I'd lost my hotel, and every other area hotel was booked.

A friend said, "I know someone," and that led to the new venue that was the perfect spot.

I tried to accommodate those who were signed up, and, as we got closer to the new date, I lost three-fourths of the people who had been registered up until the day before.

A thought of doubt flashed in my mind, but it was attacked by my dreambots.

You've spent all this money, hired a production company, and gotten sponsors. This will not be in vain.

So, I did what I do best, which is produce extraordinary results under pressure.
I hit the streets and my network, and we filled the seats again the day before the event.

Things may not go in the order that you want them to.

The job you wanted was not the job for you. The person you thought you needed wasn't the one for you. The year you felt was your year was only a time for you to reflect, not collect.

What I'm saying is this: if you have a vision or dream of being or doing something, don't be discouraged if things seem not to be working out—because they are.

You just have to remain patient, focused, and encouraged through the process of manifestation.

LEADERSHIP

Reduce your ego and watch your team grow!

When leaders' egos outweigh the contributions of their team members, mission success is jeopardized.

Self-serving leadership has proven to be ineffective in maximizing team performance. Teammates who feel they are heard, understood, and valued by their leader tend to have higher levels of commitment and job satisfaction. This ultimately leads to increased performance and productivity.

Uncommon
leadership
will produce
uncommon
results.

L.E.A.D.E.R.S.H.I.P. means:

Leverage

Every

Asset.

Develop

Every

Resource.

Set the example.

Hone

Individual

Potential.

If you have lost
the respect of your
team, your team
has lost a leader

Now that you
have the power,
it's how you wield it
that defines
your character.

A leader without a vision creates followers without a purpose.

If a leader fails to provide employees with a vision to obtain and motivation to do so, their work seems meaningless.

If you are going to
teach people,
you have to
reach people.
If you are going
to reach people,
you have to
connect with people.

If you don't understand whom you lead, then you are misleading.

A gardener understands the dynamics of plants so that they can create beautiful gardens of diverse plant species. They understand the importance of the soil in which seeds are planted, the water they are given, the amount of light they are exposed to, and the care they are provided.

Just like gardeners, leaders must understand the people they lead in order to create harmonious, high-performing work environments of diverse individuals.

Developing and improving ones' soft skills (e.g., emotional and social intelligence, communication, conflict management, and group dynamics) should be a priority for all leaders seeking to capitalize on their human capital.

Managers put people and processes in place.

Leaders show people their value amongst the places in the organization.

They will model what they follow, so let your example be upright.

We can sometimes be in a leadership position and unknowingly influence those who are following us.

In a position of influence, we have to understand the essential nature of what we do because what we do influences the behavior of others. That can be kids, friends, or employees.

We can't necessarily see how our actions impact others. Be mindful of what you do and how you do it when you interact with others.

Leadership is

about service,

not being served.

There's no true organizational performance without effective communication.
What others see is what is heard. What you say goes unseen if your actions don't line up with your words. Leaders, your actions count more than your words.

Your position
in the race
doesn't always equal
the outcome.

You might not always

be up front,

but it's good to

push from behind.

Don't try

to get into position

too fast.

You can get

burned out.

We are not leading machines; we are leading human beings.

Empathy is the key to unlock the doors of conflict. One must understand the other's perspective to resolve the disconnection.

Empathy is often overlooked as a strategic element when dealing with conflict.

During strategic war planning, we seek to understand how the opposition thinks, feels, and reacts to our actions. The same goes for day-to-day conflict on teams.

How could my actions knowingly or unknowingly affect members on my team?

The only way to mitigate this is by genuinely getting to know who's on your team. Their cultural background, communication style, work experience, and work ethic are some very important factors.

Some may think this leadership strategy is too tedious, but it is worth the investment over the long run.

Taking an authentic interest in those you work with is invaluable. Utilizing micro-moments to gather this information has more benefits than you know. Inquiring about their family, asking to learn their language, soliciting their insights, and involving them in the decision-making process develops organizational commitment and job satisfaction.

They need to know that you care and have their best interest in mind.

SOCIAL
ETHICS

Just because I'm smiling and being cordial doesn't mean I don't see the envy in your eyes.

When you are working on your self-development, you must understand that your growth will make some around you uncomfortable.

Some people want you to stay where you are so they can feel better about themselves. You may have thought they were your best friends until you began to better yourself.

This is part of the process.

Once you see the changes in them, don't let them know you see. They are confirming that you are moving in the right direction.

When you

find your way,

it's easy to show others

where you came from.

How could you appreciate the pleasure without experiencing the pain?

If the zombies are after you, that's a good sign.

Zombies only feed off the living.

People who are striving in life attract zombies: saboteurs, dream killers, and gossipers.

If you are not trying to advance in life or are hanging around nonprogressive people, the zombies won't bother you.

It's only when you begin to *live* that they become aware of your life force—and then you become prey.

Acknowledge them because they acknowledge your life potential in action.

Just don't let them catch you!

Be careful
where you
invest your
interest.

I didn't let you in because I've seen the dirt on your shoes.

When people come into your life, be sure to check their shoes.

The shoes symbolize what principles they stand on—not from a materialistic standpoint, but from their character.

Are they gossipers, scammers, liars, selfish, abusers, users, envious, etc.?

All those things track dirt, drama, depression, and disorder into your life.

My mental diet
doesn't allow for
cotton-candy
conversations.

If you are the token, make way for change.

If you find yourself as the first, make room for the second.

For whomever comes after you should have a better understanding of the environment and how to navigate it.

Runners run.

Liars lie.

Cheaters cheat.

Thieves thieve.

It's your choice

what you allow

them to do.

Believe in action and not in words because the truth is often blurred.

Many people say things that contradict their actions.

We allow the relationship we have with them to minimize the things we see them do.
Let your eyes hear the truth.

If relationships are built on anything other than trust, people will do whatever to get what they want out of them.

We are all connected and desire the same basic needs, which are to be valued for who we are and to be loved.

So, if you want it from others, give it.

Whatever you do unto others shall be done unto you.

Think twice before spitting daggers. They cut as much coming out as going in.

When you start
to outgrow your
situation,
expect those
still in the situation
to act out.

Don't judge the outside until you've gone inside.

Give a person the opportunity to show you who they are and give yourself the opportunity to know *why* they are.

Making snap judgments about people and acting on those judgments will cause you to overlook the value that's in them for you.

Our blessings come to us through us.

People

will try to make you out

to be everything

but who you

really are.

Until you decide where you want to be in life, you'll remain lost following other people's lives.

When you find yourself more concerned with other's lives than your own, it's a clear sign that you have lost your way.

People try to become other people because they lack self-value.

You have within yourself what they have within them. It's OK to use others as a reference point, but to become a carbon copy negates your sense of self.

If you want them

to grow strong,

you must feed them

with healthy life

principles and

exercise their minds

properly.

The misunderstood understands the minds of those who think they know but know not how to think.

Rumination is the cultivation of the mind's soil, but if the soil is devoid of substance, growth is stagnant.

Read books that will expand your understanding of self and others and life.

Develop relationships with people who will expand your experiences and mental boundaries.

Many of our problems stem from being surrounded by thought zombies who prey on any who dare to think for themselves.

My rights end where yours begin. You have the right to speak your mind and live your life until it infringes upon the rights of another. Now that's a different situation.

Reduce your stress and let them handle their own mess.

So many people burden their lives with the problems of others and wonder why their lives are unsatisfying.

You have to learn to let people go so you can grow.

Helping someone through something is one thing, but doing everything for them is crippling. It doesn't allow them to develop the life skills needed to be self-sufficient.

ACKNOWLEDGMENTS

I'd like to thank my mom, Irene Williams, for always believing in me, and my team for the continued support.

*9 7 8 0 5 7 8 4 0 7 5 3 1 *